Writing 28

The publication of this book was supported by a grant from the National Endowment for the Arts in Washington, D.C., a federal agency created by an Act of Congress in 1965.

Also by David Schaff

Tables

The Ladder

The Moon by Day

David Schaff

Four Seasons Foundation
San Francisco: 1971

Some of these poems first appeared in *Cassiopeia*, *Crooked Anger*, *Ephemeris* I-III, *Glide Anthology*, *Restau Review*, *War and Peace*, and *Writing (Georgia Straight* Supplement)

Library of Congress catalog card no.: 77-133240
Standard Book no.: 0-87704-017-6

The Writing Series is edited by Donald Allen and published by
Four Seasons Foundation, 1815 Jones Street,
San Francisco, California 94109

Distributed by Book People, 2940 Seventh Street,
Berkeley, California 94710

CONTENTS

Light Wheels (1970)

THE IRIDESCENT SEA

I

Undersea   a Wood
and garden   tempers
Love   past and present
in their glow   *I have seen*
at not too great a distance

from whom?
runs fair or foul of a sail
boat overturned in the shallow bay
Swamped in a stormy tide
the choice was to hold on
or kick off and wade to the mud
flat island   The choice
was to give yourself to the sea
or get out of it
Later   a sheet of rain
sawed through the islands
The storm broken

dock lay overturned
and the small sailing
craft would not stay up
It sinks to the year of other storms
apart by three summers
and to the smell of blood
in sand   I would fish
all night for lovers I knew waded
out of the sea   An envy
of the gull swept
through each run along the breakers
alone   who was I to know
what course I ran

3

Yet the sea
did not make me drunk
with more than what spun
before me   As each raft
I turned back to the jetty
I had climbed before
again to know

the fall I must have
taken but forgot
Now a fear of heights
the color of broken wood
moves beyond
the summer's fire
A man calling
for a seagull finds
no name   no echo   If
the island sank
waves at the top of
its shoal would come alive
The sail and mast ride
up as a crescent hooked
in the night sky
The Boat-of-what-shall-come
bends beyond eclipse
moves up the coast
abreast of the grey beach
sea-grey breakers
Its guidelines are

not solitary
but the sea-robes
sea-rose   and its arrow
burn near each ship
sent out to find them
And from that swirl
a gull flies toward us

II

Having died

so many times   to drive
into the story is not possible
not sure   to take you down

is not only to go deep
but for a time to be visited
undersea   'You'

walk where depth may not be measured
An image of what goes on
in negative wanders

in and out of a closed garden
In your hand a bit of incense
in your eye love glimmers

but it is not a goal
Your companion is a shell
lamp or cup

may pass from 'your' hand
under the coral ceiling
swirls past you

found near the bottom
set into your forehead
lanterns come out as peacock fish

You rise   The cold
cuts into your left side
By divination's mirror

you knit
what the sea transmutes
into a net of images

'you' transmute
the moon on its side
the tide of blood

filled with the moon's
sea-birds   Your mouth
whirls into the telephone

The magician
sails before you
Streets waver and grow dim

The veil of Wood
parts   beyond
it a deep house lingers

to the right
side a cross
'is out of place'

'The willow branch
has taken my sight
Don't ask the moon to give it back'

Above the smoke
you get no answer
Only the broken flute

healed somewhere inside you
carves each instrument from your body
'You'   wait

for sleep
to hold the air
its lightness
grown inside
the rhythm
growing from the dark
meadow
through which
friends lead you
or you lead them
No need to
beware of the night
of what flies
over   or before
the land.

III

The eye of the dead
the eye of the dead tree

half   of 'your' face
blocked by the moon

the eye of the tree
'your' hand

moves aside
the blond fern

petrified
stump unlocks its eye

open under
the slab of rock

an eye out
for the dead

blocks out half
of 'your' face

the moon
wears a cap of gold

the moon
running from the tide of

the night's tide
runs over its branches

reach for the crown
the green moon

drawn back into
the sea's shadow

eclipsed but open
the moon an eye in

the face of a man
face of the ram

the moon
opposed to it

The eye of Cyclops
blind but open

has been set
into no ram's head

The jewel
of the sea fashions

healing for
the blind   sun-struck

or driven out
The patron of the sky

still may guide his boat into
the pasture

Beyond the moon's glare
the shepherd

with one eye patrols
the wide meadow

of moon's blood
Eyes of the dead

open the white stumps
chalk ferns dancing

will not lead you from
your leading

yourself to and from
what state you wish

where the moon is rambling
across the sky and Cyclops

limps   where Hercules
throws his arrow

into upper mind
a balance is set

for each wave
of the sea's standard

'you' question
the arrow's flight

the weight
of the balanced ladder

balance of the arrow's light
The moon covers one

of your eyes
The other turns to a star

rushing towards
the white blood as it spreads outward

The moon has reached
the star

light
comes out of hiding

where
you have gone.

IV

An olive woman
a woman white as pearl
a woman of the dark
light in action

What is hurting you
and why the wine
soaked instruments of
a negative dream

you asked
a woman not present
The magician
burning in his fire
brushed back his hair
went into the next room
to let sleep
carry on his work
The moon

leapt in his window
crept to the
unguarded bed
From his silver
forehead a
dream rose
in one eye
then the next
opened
A brass key
fell to the floor
A strong box

fell apart
False hopes flew out
The chamber shrank
back inside you
curled from your marble lips
Your breasts grew
large and 'you'
touched
the sleeping hand

flowers fell from its
wire tendrils

Who could tell
from whom they had been
stolen   You rode
back out the window
The magician
followed for a second
or an hour
he did not know
When he awoke

an ore had left
its material in
him as light
Were we to love
and joke about
names no longer
the stone world
would open

The magician
found a moon
spot high
on his temple
a crescent crept
in and out of
his skull
turned as
a half-disc
or wing
his mind
completed

*Who met you
when you awoke
Who looked beyond
the mirror
into the next day?*

V

Light and dark   wings
beat the phantom   of the sun

until it collides   with the real sun
The road sweats
heat swells

beckons   the tri-
    cornered crossing
three witches under one hat
    one arch
three
spinners of mystery
    under one image
It
    is raining

you are
    driving
gasoline
    and death linger
by your side
    lurk
in the road's bending

will   'they' wait
await the changing of

the light
The sharp smell

16

of tar
and burning tires creeps
   into the vent

into the rear
   view mirror
You keep

   on driving
The light   changes
   'you'   begin

to climb up hill
   The ghost
or was it only smoke

returns to the tide marsh
Your fear takes
the wheel   keeps you

   driving
longing for the dawn

   for the sun
Have you manufactured
   it or has it come

to you on the telephone
   A burning table

wheel   and its languid spin
    pull you
once
    more into the
numerical dance
    of stoplights
gardens
    lost arcades
beneath the moon
    ruled by visitors
you have called
    are drugged
by knowledge
    of their own spin

tempt 'you'
    into the mill
you are driven
    your images
collide with

what lies beyond them
The tree   opens
Its leaves
are eyes

your eye
beyond that   of the medium

traveling   over rocks
onto a new coast

the green
hills of which
abound.

18

VI

Cut   loose
your shadow
is the moon

floats beyond
you return waving
it and wavering

at what you
have seen
the moon's

flag weaving about you
Did it hold you
and make you love what held you

The wound
of a ghostly rose
awoke in you

that anguish
you had for so
long treasured

as yours alone
as your only
object to treasure

You flung out
the torn banner
for all to see

19

how the moon would
not catch it
how the sun burned it

and you
were set free
to dance

dance and abuse
as only love could abuse
one who had known its failures.

VII

'You'   took thin fire
wandered near the center
whetted your firing rod
burnished it until
the fire sprung
white forge opened
Weather   each madness
or season unfolding
heat   of the ladder
is blue fire
is anger
outstretched

turns
'you'   the horseman
by night riding from campfire to
camp   fire   under the horse surrounds
you bring a corral of light
into the burnt circle someone
who does not recognize
the crowned script of what you carry
salutes   'your' intelligence
outskirts her   You

are the Water Bearer
ashamed that you carry
the Moon
carries you off
on the Perilous Road
'you'   as Virgo   'inter Virgines'
near the center

a wind bats each Virgo with a radio
a wing dates you never past never present
your obsession   with burning
with the rungs and nets of being
you burn
at the foot of the Wooded Mountain
the Lamp of Memory

when green night lasted
the sea rose around
the moon's iron tower
those who manned it
held semaphore
robes of light   and carnage
hung out as battle laundry
Don't spill the water
Don't turn off the radio
you felt yourself hooked to
earphones   and propellors of
a fiery grail

VIII

Not in Neptune's Palace
where undersea gardens move
shift   forever
vacant foliage
travel so immense
we dissolve in its
dream of how far
how long to keep on going
bend desire for
love fits which crooked bow
boomerang you launch
Your flesh will
will not heal   'you' travel
without end   but always at a high speed
is there rest

a halfway point
along the coast near
the end of the sugarlump
hills   sketched-out by
which to note where
to go and where not
runs into the gardener
in whose green arms are gnarled
bits of tree   bits of clay
He carries coal
and mother of pearl
from the sea-fields
coral flowers fall
from the shimmer above your head

You are turning
in your sleep
remember
love by accident   By
the Waters of Occident
you sat and wept
Tears of that midnight were
jewels in Neptune's Palace
when next you entered
a rainbow of despair
hung about 'your' neck
You will find no rest here   you said
The next morning awoke in admonition.

IX

The trellis
from the ground floor to
the second story had
gone so long without repair
none of us knew
when the short clamps
had been set
into the downstairs'
porch columns
From the second story
you swung out

into the branches
down   into the thorns
'You'   had broken
the flowers' unpainted
crossbar and
rusted wire
had climbed into
desiring arms
the blue flower
beneath a rock
and golden bird
that did not work for you
but journeyed

beyond the garden
where windings would not reach
beyond the Wood
where deception's
embedded riches lie
From their speech
a stranger flew
before the gate
of forest and meadowland
undersea   Mellowed by
the sun no longer
the green bronze of spears
measured the garden in

the *Wood*
you are trying to escape
caught   you watch
your house
travel on the night
You go
beyond the garden
enter   the room of
ships and birds
And with the hands of love
you reach into the shadows
to tear the shutters down.

X

Don't ask the moon to give back
the eye of the dead
the moon's eye

drowned man's dreaming
or his ecstacy
lost within as he looks to

whatever you have searched
something flies beyond
the effort at flight

carries you to the sea-cave
of a man beside himself with
coals of misunderstanding

throws down the chain
being ties to flesh
the wind may separate

or tie   its ribbons firmly
You thought of the passage
where the cave turns outward

a city blooms
the man of the sea
no longer one-sided

is at one with the elements
of his flight
The boat

and storm traveling together
reach new lands
Words at their outset

no longer bind them
Look where you may
on the other side

of the hill the woods
are fair and filled with ferns
Streams become clear

as pebbles at their bottoms are
washed to gold   the pure
elements of the sea are gathered in

what is washed in and washed out of
the hurricane's eye   *the moon*
like a ship's prow steers through the clouds

You were riding
an old but trusted car
not alone with the sea

before you had been
unaware of
fog and wind you contact

but have no means of interrupting
For an instant the dead may stop
then return

Who stands before you
dials long distance and will not
reply   You

asked for and were given
certain gifts and
uncertain fortune

separate fleets
they sailed as one
out of the harbor

into the light
At first you looked for
a dark woman

then searched for
a joining of impossibilities
Bound by revenues

in a sky you could not reach
in a wound you could not bind
only the blood is real

the Beast does not haunt
but will uncoil beneath
Angels of Brutality

tie the City to
hunger   convulsion
you are almost unable to believe

the sea
will not die
a city

may spin and break
the flood erupts
subjects

the green hills to
sulphur   The mills
work overtime   overflow   'You' hope

that it is all a trading post
at worst a pawnshop   Will the sea
cover and heal   Will the earth

you are left asking
as the ground pulls away from you
careening
around the dark side of the moon
are rings like those of Saturn
bound to a common diameter
they untie the sea-cords
flames of ruined desire
and runes of moon-faced sand dollars
you cannot spend or read properly
Are you able to
take the moon
from its rectangle of
divided silence
You careen
about the dark side
hope to reach the light

In the arms of unknown birds
will the copper disk
traveling with you
open the trade winds
flight lines of the sea-falcon
'You'   fall
into what you imagine
rebounding infinitely
until the dark edge of the moon
opens to free you from
the sun in coarse blankets
covering the city

'You'   attempt to describe
what you are partially responsible for
                transmuted before
or after you have touched it
                        Seer
or sea-and-land rover
you get up to
                uncover the City
take down the blankets
that mask the moon

                        Later
you reached for the car's
side-mirror
What you thought was
the moon
became the dim headlight
of an old Ford
driven by one of three girls
into your blind spot

31

it then shot ahead of your
looking for another moon
Why had you lost this one
or gained it in so curious a way
it was gone
You drove on home
A word or two
crept over the hood
folded into the radio
the arbitrary nature of
how you kept on driving

at last reach home?
You go to a table
on which lie a shell and a stone
You pick them up
the cup of one
almost fits the concave patternings
of the other   The stone
is a glass bird
The shell has Cufic script
carved into the name of God
or of an angel
The bird
with a shell on its back
reminds you of the Moon
not out tonight
made love to a stone
locked a sun under clear rock
The moonstone grew
          into the Stone of Scone
crown of faery kings
no gold nor silver
floated above the Gaelic King

You
are a Priest
after the Order of Melchizedek

you heard
you were entrusted with
no temporal kingdom
but the shell's glow

      "I cannot know
the faeries
dancing on Tamalpais
the faery prince   who grants
prayers given at Shasta

      I have too little
Celtic blood   too little dancing
      I who am half bird
half bear
      go over the mountain

I desire
but may only love
a woman whom the Moon has given to me

the names of wizards
in the Celtic or the Gaelic tongue
      I am not sure"

> Again the Moon
> comes in the window   *May*
> *I follow*
> *Where are you and what have you given*
>   *that now is taken away?*

The stone
overturned again
falls from the sea-falcon's back
in the dark river
a boat grows up to catch it
Europa and the Bull
glide beyond their lunar guidance
Below them
The King of Ocean and of Rivers
lies in troubled sleep
His heart
flutters like the Doomsday Book
He sees darkly
where poisoned arrows
uncurl from faery bows
women and moon-pages
uncurl the glimmering wood
At its center
are two trees
a road to the moon goes between them
runs beyond
your house with a single light
weighing down the arms of an oak
From it you hear

the Poet-Prince
his crazy dancing
faery   babble
nothing but
faery   marvelings
bubble from his fountain

Will they answer
or allow you to move on through the moon's eye
from the sea
into silence
of the blue flower
broken teak table
and folksy painted bowl
You think clearly
of those you love
almost hear them
talking of what
they value most
and how to preserve it
from what they desire least.

The iridescent sea
lengthens   and grows dim
'you' said

you were conscious of
a fire
a music in

all that approached
went beyond the breakers
'you'   joked

about the shell
desire had
thrown on the rocks

wound about
the hard facts of
the sea's life

drove 'you' mad
In the lunar year
you had four

'good days'   blazed
as the sea pierced
dark rock   the serpent's

power floated
The shell grew wild
soft weeds

held it to the shore
the dim horizon
Now in your eye

a peacock
and sea gull battle
A dream will win

and what you knew
will become accomplishment
beyond its flower

will it continue
or go under
the evening sea.

The Wood

anvil   Fire
wood and stone
The heavy air

texture of
the dock   Pushed
out into the night
you drift
The fog
watches over
the rocks
will not catch you
until you wake
The room sways
its light
brings a boat's lantern
Unlit shore

curls from you
into the painted image
out of the painful landscape
branches are
broken at their elbows
no blood
but cottages lie vacant

Their lights move
upward you look
into men on a wheel
Who has sewn shut
their boutonnieres
Who has wound tight
their wounded hearts

your heart?
You share
the wine of the sea
sea-fire
shale and wood
rise above
pine trees wavering
before their mountains
From the boat
you step on land
            are met
by a woman
riding from the moon
by her opposite
gliding over the waters
by Love
or what you had called love
dancing
            before you
on clear hills
in clear day
dancing
            with you
forcing you
into the music
into the dancing

you come laughing
Will the world live
what world lives
below
        above
Try to name
try to acquire

       Fish
air   stone   Fire

The wood net breaks to let them through
opens a garden
the garden   undersea
but there   here unfolding.

DEDICATIONS

Annals

The horns of
          the town
a garden
          of Pennswoods

settled 1744
predominantly, from the center
of Philadelphia formerly
known as the City-of-Brotherly-Love
16 miles to

Wayne
formerly known as
"Louella"
renamed for

Mad Anthony
around 1800, bramble growing
met by the horns of
roses, by 1900
now are the most fragrant in
Pennswoods
across the street

the Finley Memorial House
1789, constructed
in the time of Governor Morris
1964, given by
Miss Dorothy Finley

no mention of
an oracle   here or elsewhere
in Philadelphia, though the Liberty
Bell, tone of Independence Square's
old houses near the Delaware
are near the mark

none remain in
"Louella"
In Philadelphia
Ben Franklin's
statue is covered
in pigeon crap, metal
beneath events

fountains, Fairmount
Park and Strawberry Mansion,
below which concerts are held
          in Robin Hood Dell, below
which the river
Schuylkill runs,
full of silt, caking the hulls of
shells, small boats and pleasure craft
at liberty to pull up at
clubs by the green river bank

          into biographies
of Bittle or Barnes   here
politics are as in other moneyed places
stale   but 'there are good people'
about to take over Morris'
chair?   The butt of ale
in John Bull's cellar, my friend

Mike Bull's father, last year
gave way to bottled beer; farther
in Pennswoods are mills, clover
mill and grain, covered bridges
Colonial houses, rural pomp, ca. 1750
–1850, down to
1900, say 1930, more wealth, steal
and the whirl of debutantes
held up by
the gentle crust
of cobwebs hardening
or becoming pure silk
There's no mail for
an oracle
should be a patriarch
of this city
but of late is uninvited

The fibers of constitution are now webs.
What metal figure breaks them?
The blades of railroad tracks,
mills, barns, cars, free-
ways, churches
and supermarkets
are not shining. The roses
heavy in their velvet plumage
fall;
they will bloom next year
The cemeteries

are horns of
a constant spinning
William Penn
married to Betsy Ross,
Lancaster and York
lie deeper in Penn's Woods
Replaced by city dancers
they do not give up a balance of
the flower and the web
Year after year
"Louella"

leaves the dead-letter office
The bell
in Constitution Hall hangs motionless
The city
full of abuse   (settled Theos)
is rebuilt,
neighborhoods change, some die, others
come forward, blood
is renewed
but does not seem to change

a webbed city
        green touched by grey
trees are full grown but more grow
awkwardly
        The house across the street
glitters only in twilight
The geography is full

        opens the road to
the city's shimmering,
the fall of
        the Delaware River,
Spring and
        Fall annals of
recorded years.

July 1967

Intents

Birds   are ideas of place
landing   call

that the perch holds
grain has fallen

landing bird
called from the air

delayed in fire
frequent disguiser

of nearness, you are
what is reaching you   Now

        the shadow of
plague   years
new wounds opening in
        the movement towards man

cover scars
beneath them fire breaks out,
        how deep does anger move
rises through grey
        streets smeared
with soot and blood, whirls in

              blood-purple
Asphodelia, blood-Hecate of Newark

blooming
            girders
twis-
      ted skyline, life-
land,
      where are the

meadows   (of spiritual love)
I would not enter
            one step before my time
now one step behind it looking   looking

            from some hill
            a cavern opens

            the under-road
            cut-off hinges of

            hell's balcony
            —will assert a gravity

            to pull down stars,
            the price of which

            yanks at
            webs of the invisible

            through which tanks crawl,
            myrrh-maids eaten

offered nothing
but misapplication,

there's no intention
here, sirrah

just rotting,
yet impenetrable

as the glow of Zenon
or radiation
the djin of the morning
stalk the parks at night,
see them
sporting in your heart,
what's in first
place there, a line of stags

waiting for action,
now Acteon

pulls down Antares,
shot

through with mortality
the abstract kills

the white city,
it might be San Francisco
and I thought of
no white monastery
panthers, who will eat fruit

the scarred wings
draw upward, whatever

it is struggles, are we
prey on that back or guiding it

returning from
under-waters
a boat slipping out of
unnamed harbors
draws our warring after it.

The Horn of

for Richard Roth (1941–1966)

The Knight of Swords
The Queen of Cups

a pocket full of
          grain
beyond wheat fields
          the trumpet

sweet grain
from the horn of

          the four desires:
one for heaven   two for love
          one for death

To bridge these four
you wanted
to get out of the ruin

a fifth desire
pours bodies into
          the mill of age
a dark grail

attendants administer
This cup will raise you
You shy from all contact
Swallow this eye of white peacock
the movement towards light
Shallow the eye when knotted against you
Not in monastery
or in the knot if flesh alone
winding through
each visit
is the cup   *which end?*
which means?   raised to
the hard angle of
sweet and bitter grain

Nor is the fall
continuous
        sun-baked
sun-raised

There are two desires for love
apart from all else
one   is enough if found
Shallow the cup when not filled
to the lip
this curved life
full of visits   loving
not only pleasure
but burning   the waves
black bird at the window
the grail spills
longing
This cup would fill
Silent

for death's longing
drove where you wanted to go
you went
I am certain the way held a thread
of or to you seemed one path to
Paradise   *Words are grain*
the sun-caked road
you did not stop on   I sat in
could say nothing   *would I ever go*
the house emptied   *eternity*
as tilted as before   Your guitar
moved through the city
(Love)
whose destructors
are brothers to those who made it

the Djin
enter   another house
your visions are no different
the knife
at the night window
sword and magnetic radio turning over
the window is your melody
accompanies black birds and their speaking with
a ruined drum   The lid opens

A woman makes you turn
her name into an absolute
You spoke
of what had ceased to move within you
moves in
No space   no time
the dark   singing windows of

glimmering before the thread
of unknowing
you had so often granted yourself
love
from which no release came
you laughed to receive
permission
I am now present in

May this record:
your spirit made of flame
avail desire and her messengers
the horn sword of memory
avail words attendant on your light
to rise   beyond their inscription
May your name not fall

The unstrung question
lies in the road bed
first cup
of grain
          there are movements
the pouring grain
          is register of

a field   trumpet
          (a *City*)
attendant   and given.

Memoir

A hawk
    (I am a hawk)
A bittern

wings set far to the rear
  head and breast
thrust forward

soars above
  the freeway
In the picture

you had just put up
  an osprey
untangled branches

looking for
  an unknown foe
The bittern

changed in flight
  wings curled
into horns

and the moon drove
  a Ram before
it in and out of focus

     I thought of
Jack   with a notebook
   and a glass of brandy
Robin spoke

of what moved
     an image   not an ideal
in   talk of Jack
     there was Jack

in the wire of words
     birds clutching bottles
I among them

and whoever went looking for
Jack found longing
I went to the bar awhile back, found

     birds caught in
swinging doors.
     When Jack died

I thought of a genie in a bottle,
that at least there would be no carcass
though a vulture feasted on light from Jack's table

for the wealth had gone
I had seen a part of it

Whoever went longing
found what he looked for,

a pale light ringing the table
a fluttering in the bar—

As I came here,
    invited to late dinner,
Jack's fable

    fell into place.
This food
    is blessed

casually
    the image breaks
Robin spoke   You   answered

what constant-
                ly seemed
impelled outward.

with Don

Harvest

—for J. M.

The well   who leapt
yields
            broken pottery
leaping   small fish into
small rock pools
                    The sea
harvest of the red sun
do not sail its morning
last night the same sign
would have been fortunate
now malcontent
Don't fake your leaping
language in your turning of its
fiery motion   serpents
and sea angels   the sea words
sea worlds   ascend and descend
no limit to their number
no limit   to your leaping
                        Yours
is the host's fortune
where the sun baked nihil of words
fall into the grain of
coherent time   You have made safe
the iridescent ladders
plain and steps of the sea wall

You have entered
the co-ordinants of prophecy
and returned with them at your command
        Do you move when
daemons also intelligent of the ladder
attend
       To even a daemon
you may accord good fortune
that truth   blaze in the world
that evil   return to its citing
and never leave the mark

  May your desire
return all contents of desire
and from these shards
you know the style of.

November 1967

No seer alights
higher than this image
fallen from a star
earth seen from that distance

revolves, sure
there's a double axis
—where are you from
turning each night to your window

sweet as a meadowlark
afraid of the light?
In that community
you visit in your astral self

a light burns continuously,
a small beacon but incessant
tonight it wavered in drunkenness
your voice twisted

as it flew out the window
but found itself unimpowered
diverse spheres,
one point may seem the crystal of,

against symmetry, the plant's thriving
Tie up its flowers,
unwind them
as you would let your heart
be bound.

The Birth of Venus

*on the birthday
of Robin Blaser
18 May 1968*

The island
afloat in your dream
wakes in your hand

Accept   no less
than what you wanted
all to cohere in

a knowing of the paths
closed and open
Still your trip

was not canceled
Onward you journeyed
until you met

the slender foot
of a spell-formed mountain
No way up

someone from a high
perch said
The fourth and last

migration from Atlantis
brought you here
The dimension of Paradise

you may not escape
or escape into fully
is in this life

an island
shell thrown
from the sea

through imagery
could be anyplace
you travel to

without leaving home
in the boat of the dream
image of the heart

there is no idyll
but fruition
You have almost traveled

through the eye
of Spirit's needle
fruit and fire

escape your hands
They crown your sight
You are the gate

of pleasure and of sorrow
The blood of garnet
wound into

a priestly coat
is your robe
for knightly travel

your cape
of sea flowers
you turn and face us from

Who stands beside you
or inside
your outstretched arm

Call her Desire
Love   or what you will
she is in all hearts

and from that music
incessantly moving
she steps

to your embrace
You are given
the cup of fortune

and of time
All who drink there
know its wonder

the shining figure of desire
approaching   and forever theirs.

Acrostic

DARIEL
URIEL
RAPHAEL
DAZIEL

In midst of fire
an underhanded moon
reached out to heal
and spreading through
the meadow-room
robes of orange entered
unheeded wandering
until a new life found them
Their monastery
was a factory
all its figures
binary sequence of the mind
Floating on the outside
to hold a demon inside
insert your head
into the forehead of the power,
then animate
eyes you may not know
Tidal evening will
grow when fed with fire,
the poor demon
become a principle,
or some causality
with blood as well

65

Do not depend on water
or on metaphor
Light covers all as we know it
The mind may discover
as much as it does not know.

Voyage

to David Bromige

Evening
and a melancholy flute
fold over me. A fog
close to drunkenness
but not too close warps
a drug of long abstraction
through my sleep

Blue sea, blue sky, crimson moon
—from one person to another
'Yes I've a violin to play you'
The coffee pot is brown
'My heart is umber'
I found you and the negro girl
beyond the crumpled house,
the red orchid
clouded evening

Near a grey
sea-wall later an alien pulled us
A wet wind pushed from the East
and though we did not leave
the speckled street board
nothing kept us
on land
You were probably at home
I was in New York

and took the next train out
My head seemed a hanging plant
nonetheless I wrote
you about rummaging around a stone park
got home cut my hand on
a drawer I unraveled
then went to sleep on the couch.

The Prophet

for Robert LaVigne

That the spirit burn free from the fire
you have carried torches
on ship and on land
have moved through the night

daytime passage
on the ferry between worlds
you have worn smooth the decks
carved from the wood of both realms

beyond which
the sea is not at rest
beyond which
is territory without attributes

you map
shells to cross over
To return or not
is your choice

your territory   The moon
is a third eye
The sea like a well
opens beneath touch

carries the hand beyond water
The eye in its palm
looks for light
flickering beyond the door

no less than mind
becomes water
bearer, bird or extent
Rest is momentary

form then changing form
unsought but present
the eye

longs to marry the moon
give her away to dancing
You arrive on its measure

burn the rafts of intelligence
A word beyond your voice
unlocks the tide and its moon-robes

swirl around you
Ferried to a land of never finishing anything
you return as one who can make

the soul cohere
though their destruction is complete
no last touch paws at your images

or reaches into our mouths when we relate
how flesh may cross time
unlimited   by what were clearly limits in time

You have unlocked pleasure's gate
through the outskirts of memory
you have moved intent on healing

all that is broken by desire
you have lifted into a higher mind
held its mirror and walked through it

carrying what burns undersea
into your language   Whatever implements
were necessary you received

To discard the means of art
enter a valley of what is undescribed
How you go and return

is a wafer dumb in our mouths
Does your kiss numb them further
or open the heart

You have put aside
the cup of iniquity
black tray of ill-made fortune
Carried by your wings

the water-banner may discard its windings
becomes unbound beyond our eye
Above the house of the reborn
does a field of prophecy

or one of labor
throw itself around the house-frame
of your light made of water
tears thrown down as impure gold.

The hard ore
flies before sorrow
as before ecstacy
From it we learn

what must be real
variations of which
run near the blood
through it   shared
are ever yours.

15 July 1968

because of Dan Moore and the Floating Lotus Magic Opera

Divine Lotus
alive on the waters
White   Flower
of the Abyss?
of the distance
between perception
and paradise
A floating island
you surround us
your vapor is our blood
your embrace
what we know of
Ecstacy.

But why call
in an abstract voice
Wind and fire
affect you
as any physical body
you follow gravity
and the sun
heals what ills you reach
You are pure
of self-undoing
The heart finds

in you a perfect arc
Drunk on emptiness
desire sounds in
the chanter's palm
A line of trees
waves before your meeting
death and its
many colored opposites
You go beyond
unknowing   and out of it
you lead us

your companions
open to you
and to your movements.

Salutes

(Under ALGOL)

—for Lewis & Lew

Those who are possessed
     possess

  Shaman
    demon
      beggar
   king
undersea blind
       seer
  in command of

the coil of gold
foil of sex

     we are
  those instruments
        weapons
or healing
     we are
  looking

for the body of love
    lantern-crossed
  the pale flesh
caressed by words   it

                    dies   lives
       Hold off striking

who will raise
           it word to mouth
mouth   to mouth   pull
the heart into motion

Sick   of all
alien beings alive within

   (also)   desire
   decaying masquerade

why do you hide
      behind those shrubs
   some god
                   longs to kill
you   dance you to pieces

part of it
apart   who
will be recognized
       from the antler-
             headdress
   headrest
will not appear
             but in metaphor
pulls the work over

   you are   free to
      know
what is known and known not

to advance under
covered hands

Tear down the masks
Tear off the blinds

   beyond both
you travel
   Have you

found an eye
   at the end of
the path or dream?

18 December1968

Politics

for George Stanley

'You might as well get into it because
you're not going to get out of it'

By *it* you meant
flesh   and its opposites

thin notes
on a roulette wheel

confusing one 'you'
with another

I rode off to the Fillmore
In the middle of a set my eyes
weren't mine but closed they wandered

to you   Cloudy
you answered   'I

don't believe in meta-physics.
By the word is meant *after*'

I spun off, could not
make it there or make sense

You were in the bar
I lay on the dance floor
with no wheel but this:

a dark sun
in the center of a card
around which a herd circles and dances

blank
to no-one reading
black
to a hand unyielding
Set into a forehead
upset and flowing over oilcloth
blood at the root
blooms matched reaching inside you
red or *read* or *red*
It is laughter

a door you won't lock
accumulating power
through ungirded windows.

Blood Star

I was born under a clouded star.
Am I never to reach the upper air
Not to accept the conditions of I am,
Perpetually to struggle or be bound?

So cosmos is born out of chaos
or the other way around, one is born
another begins to die
            The argument
about violence cannot be a peaceful one
Or can it? All the other way around
sail moons on which blood has recently been
discovered   Beyond the car window
the electric town is incredulous. Can half
the population be ill? Are you right
or left handed? The other side collects
cosmos and chaos, a snake within
a mandala, cord between worlds.

           No lineage?
A bell of blood uncurls in your voice.
Do you hear?
Here an undertone unravels chain driven
wheels interlocking,
melted down clatter in looming work,
crisscross, radar, an immense steel tower
concealed by a turnpike. Birds
fall from it. News of battle
wounded flashes through them, meadowlark and thrush
add to the news. Noise.

Radios stop. Weary
of unbroken instruments they stand before us whimpering.
Owls.
Ill-at-ease. Gates of fire
that take
no bloom. Square moons
burn on the interior, we are divided.
Trees crack. Clay-footed birds
beneath them uncurl a deadly singing
smoking bell,
turned upside down draws fire.
Its neighborhoods increase.
They are foundries,
a ghetto, into whose slow turn
everything magnetically creeps.

The song wavers. Priapus will stumble,
hold onto a blurred number. Why
do what you are doing? But the will
to remember no longer has a number.
Thumbs down.
Heads up.
Weep. For the yellow dead are resurrected,
carrying silver cups they embrace
Madness, incoherent I can no longer see you.
Who could tell where so many faltered,
few gained.
Our martyrs,
some fight back tears, some fight
back tear gas, fall into whoever will help them.
They get up, are shaking hands, each
has a cup, into which light molds
the tips of giant fronds of rainbows.

Orchestra pounds.
Some merge
hands, banks, mortalities, so ill-wounded they cannot move
but pitch themselves against grappling hooks, hauled onward
a few stripped of all else stammer to a deity. Bayonets
poorly guided, they have beaten
their brains to lead.

No lineage?
Held together only by language. Flowers of brass,
the metal goes back, sinks into the ground.
The caldron relaxes. In the same country,
the land and road fall off to the right.
A stream runs under a covered bridge. Birds
of shallow forest land nest in rafters
half hardened into stone. To the city,
fourteen miles. The valley flows southward.
A dream instructed those who held to the land
to build an immense disc shaped against
the rock, shaped towards the heavens, to collect
all forms of light. To bring them inward.
Filled with some light, we proceed as if by sonar
gathering magnitude and field.
Open, outward, the caldron is a magic circle.
All who enter there are unbound, all centered
in that radiance drive maroon hawks before
their discovery as a shield and sun guard. They are

together, drawn into a dance of universe, a city
so formed breathes in each inhabitant. All
are citizens. And were. A continual folding outward
of what is gathered in. Unbroken

by what is always breaking. Each day
wakes again
to leave its splendid curse about
those who have bound or torn it.
Lead prayers dissolve to liberate their weavers.
And those
who have gathered light are free to weave,
increased, are able to return
elements of which they are the working,
clear from

blood star,
days without end. Everywhere beauty
sends out explosions to reach you,
missed, present but unattainable, we meet
not love, then love, turf bleeds, cloud
stairs wandering turn outward.
Hordes battle over sacred
quicksand. Wars tear at the heart,
but from that center
whose visions collapse or no longer are sustained
an unbroken singing goes.
Violet tones

stain our movement. The disc
moves forward. And will continue to move.
A thousand pure lamps flutter in unknown eyes.

If sex were the lure
of these unhappy streets alone
I'd leave them laughing.
You haven't been anywhere but desire's
one-legged messenger
hops after you to hit
you and you alone with his
flowered crutch. The Lure
pulls the devil into heaven,
will it pull us into life?
And what lure,
if Christ is only a catchword
you and I and others
go fishing from and for
an abyss filled with miners' lights.
The diamond
is what we are seeking
more often than not, love seeks us
and we will have none of it.
A bunch of funky Persians
bearing books and tasty-cakes
come to a delicatessen
and there you are
asking the animals of the forest
to come join your banquet.
But none leave
their contentment for your longing
And why should they?

You draw closer to
disappearing than the veil
meadowlarks in hell
draw between flesh and what would crush it.
Where you linger
unnetted stars gather rain into
a runic lightfall.
For there's but one like you in bliss
and few again in wisdom.
Pressure does not lift
curves from your reasoning,
flowers from your mouth.

20 May 1969

The Park

As love had been a part
of torment, a part of me left
whomever I loved, wandered
without aim or violently
—at a dark wood's edge
tearing after twilight
until I treasured moments
when away from myself I flared
after someone I could not have.
Wandering I found you.
unleashed the force I gathered.
You would not wear it, gently
took down masks—as I tore through events.
Who were you? Why was something
I did not know could move
moving? Trembling I reached
to touch you. There was no anxiety,
tenderness flowed into
my hollow hands.
A new kind of love?
I had almost forgotten
when I found myself embracing
ghost figures, ghost dancing.
Though we are as unlike
as any two people I've seen joined,
come with me.
                    For we now share
a house and a beginning.
I go out to watch stars,
really to look for owls.

It is a clear sky, a hill and
pasture are held short
by live oak clumps. The valley
is slender at this end, green
hills now umber wind toward the city.
And the early evening wind
brings the scent of plum,
uncared for trees with oblong fruit,
I look up into one, notice
one of those rare hawks
that cry from the eucalyptus.
I want to be lost, voluptuous
and tender is the woman I am seeking
—no longer to be obsessed by
a demon or angel I have always
fought through someone to reach
—no longer to travel on
unclear sight through chaos.
We need not linger there
but live in natural love.
Circles of our worlds so interlocked
that spinning there is infinity
where the sea echos, a city
gleams.
          A lost park
appeared to me as a model.
As the rooms and landscape focused
parts I had held abstractly
became mine to touch.
You brought the model. It was
no longer in miniature, or apart
from the time we are alive in.

We had made this journey often,
it seemed we knew the valley
but had I been there with you
always by the green pool?
You came down the hill
burning mists from the shallow vale.
Light wings flared from your eyes,
light branches waved behind you.
May I reach out to touch
what I know is as visionary
as my own eye, blue and scarlet
set there for a moment linger
in the negative power of memory?
But you continue toward me,
the grass in which you slightly stumble
springs up after you pass.
Your hair falls in front of
your cheek as you brush it
from your sight, intent on
your footing, on mine as
I approach you, there is flight
in our embrace. We are drawn into
a dance of orchard and roadside.
                    Let us go
into what we are to enter,
a gateway, it is open, a key to
more than what now we know.

Emissaries

What is holy?

The sweet   rock sounds
its lifeless call   I am
the universe
Dreamt of becoming
all you were in the instant of your birth
I will not lie to you
or tell you

Who I am
you are also
the morning of the hawk
a silver night and slow beginning

will enter you
for the time you do not abuse
or turn to
it as defensive art

Take courage, you may give
and accept challenges
if you are in the vicinity
they will accompany you brittlely
until you know them
the curses cities have taught you
will wander mis-
directed. Take them to you,
from their forms
your heart will lighten

each interruption,
conscious that it takes you,
you take it
this
     way and that, but if
it is
where you are to go, go gladly
Otherwise it
     is n minus x
miles back and not easy

what you are longing to discover
that what you encounter
beneath the words holds

What country shall we belong to
To what country shall we be loyal
Have you wandered between clear sight
Heard the cars and harmonies
Equally in each song?

November 1968—September 1969

LIGHT WHEELS

Winter

And when he came home
after so long at wandering
he knew only where he was

not what had been. All
he had accomplished vanished.
He sat a little astonished.

The elements were disassembled,
all his favorite knots
united, or at least misshapen.

He attached a silver leaf
to his chin—looked out
the oval uneven window.

He was living comfortably,
with almost enough for each
want at night cried to him

—he knew what he could of
their secrets. How was it they
undid or contained more?

Like a bell in the woods
something told him to plant
what would grow. A grove

fixed, or slightly wavering,
stiffening, there you might hang
or undo what you wrongly did.

Sight was difficult in
winter's mane, but his heart
rang in the budding branches.

He cared for them as for all
objects, treasuries, absorptions,
you are cursed if you follow without heart.

Visions have their co-ordinates, and the wind-swept
hills of any back country tell us why
a few men came down out of them to live.
But it wasn't enough, somewhere prophecy
wandered off, would not become property. Only to know,
even to know—what continued from what
stops. Finding your way back along the trail
you traveled in and out of chaos, of caves, in
and out of birth—at last the light continued
to flash around you. You caught its
brilliance. Caught the original glyphs of vision
in whatever hieroglyph they had found.
That flux is eternal, you proved with a pair
of broken glasses. And all changed,
if not to something greater than it was,
at least to something different—uncontained.
All roads lead, every man might become
all he might be. To each you gave. On every road
you traveled, breathlessly, breathlessly, open
handed, open eyed, open to each world.

for Charles Olson
30 January 1970

Hypnotic music
to bind everyone to dancing.
Not getting all we want
we insist on continuing
until there is no end
but a road bending back
upon itself. A broken bell
is trapped in its beauty
but does not harm the earth.
'Nor will I' resounds from
each separate well. Unlike
the bully whose brains are
at the end of a club,
up rooted
                    without bloom,
he kicks down doorways,
must have blood
—you were to go out
but find you are wounded.
You go to the window.
Outside is a flowering tree
with leaves like scales.
On its lovely arms
hard fruit's been grafted
—or it is a dying stump
forced to become bright,
whose blossoms then freeze
and are hacked off for
thorny firewood?

                    Shuffle
of newspapers—no one rhymes.
Archaic trumpets crack,
calling us to the hunt
where no-one may recognize
anyone but an enemy.
A party on the way to hell,
but in the middle of the shouting
it's suddenly time to go home
—at least someone motions
us over to look at more
than the interminable smoke.
Who is looking back?
'Is it really you?' Traveling
by train, touch, or memory alone,
each station
                    may be an island
—a small world radiant
in most directions.
There everyone dances,
wounded and eager embrace,
and when you get time to reflect
the images you have explode.
Yet an intense clarity
regathers. Wind-spun notes
shimmer like minute leaves.
Everything is tipped
in fire—as though on waking
you discover you are in love.
We may invent coherence—
even when time breaks
up, a change is granted

all who are free of
nights without mooring.

Islands,

Boats, patches of sunlight on deep water.
You stopped the car by the small dock
across from the sea raven rookery
where a meadow tapers into the inlet.
I had watched crystal drops flow up
the hood, over the windshield. You drove without
wipers—and without mistake. Images
flew past: I was dying in many of them.

I had told you of finding the wrecked car
and two bodies at the country road's end
—one moved barely and the driver groaned
from where he had landed in a ditch.
The wretchedness of dying was a dark base—
against it everything moved. Yet to be gone
and the two men found at the accident did
not move beyond their impersonal sting.

Friends, some as boats of luminous dead,
appeared in talk. To watch was to be drawn
by light that spread from prism to prism.
All touched by that fine laughter shone.
When you pulled up before the dock I felt
a dream which had clung to me like a wound
dissolve. We got out in streaked haze,
found hooks of the day about us as the wind.

to Colin Stuart
18 March 1970

98

What are the arrows?

Hoods of light, collected from address books,
unbound, scattered calendar pages
cluttering the air with bits of color.
Days. A spring binding—a
bow

drawn. Feathers
of the arrows are multicolored—let go
light passing through them as they fly
enchants the target. Transfixed,
then fixed. The quills shut

their whirling roulette.

I had taken the bow
into an open field, left it unstrung—

returned in a few weeks to find it unaltered
or so little changed the mastery I held
on it seemed identical. The bow

of dogwood. Arrows
of ash. A whirl of feathers
spiraled about the shaft, the tip with

its tilt and point of brass. Fired
at a red wall
an arrow hooks into the brick

then lodges in soft earth beneath it. Shoots
and amber leaves appear.

As if the sun were bleeding through clouds
but had been unable to break them, an eye
with the sun behind it, radiant—

Four crowds in a wide valley.
For each crowd a golden man is leader.
A black angel with six wings calls antiphon.
The crowd moves between two points.
Throwing aside all but the strongest dancers,
the leaders move, tip and feather of a weathervane.

As the body in bed
swings out to its full extent,
a giant seed about to break into flight.

Cards

Or was it bamboo
fishing pole that brought back
stained by afternoons on the deck
sitting at a table by the dance floor

—awake at five in the morning
not much to do but talk to someone
who may only talk back in memory
'For it's then'

              the voice continues
something it had stopped saying
or you had stopped listening to,
now hear clearly.

But the face, distinct in the early
dream traffic is gone.
You are rowing with someone
but the metal oars are broken.

The letters O R bat their way across bar-talk,
mockery so gentle it no longer hurts—
to know you were talking to someone you could not know.
Lights were furious.

Cars rushed up from Broadway.
Everyone turned toward a pair of dissolute children.
Words flutter up, loose-leaf, as shingles
or air-borne puff pastries

—until they were a nest of sputtering birds
caught in the new log in the fireplace,
a pair of horns, fire
turning them into chrysanthemum branches—

Why look on dangerous beauty?
Or is the nuisance of poetry
driving you to a murder?
Now politics is the lowest form of boredom

and there we are,
tied down under a myriad of overhead wires.
Each streetcar flashes by with its baggage.
There in an ad for flowers the girl

in the yellow dress poses
in front of the run-down trolley station,
Actaeon, onetime drugstore cowboy
and longtime newspaper reader, searches

but no hound pack may appear unless
those fru-frus at the bus stop draw
fandangos from their purses,
enter the trolley stop dancehall at great speed.

Or not at all. Bondage.
Bandage
the wounded stag with feathers.
And what if a sore

now so nude and festering
became unplastered from his flesh
and he took off his horns
and wrapped you in his beauty?

103

Beyond Recall

Remorse intrudes, like a fever.

The hood pulled tightly over your ears
you wander without aim through an imaginary snowstorm.
Each flake is a misconstructed act—
the years fall away, your flesh is young corn
and you stand naked with the first one you loved.
Yet she is indifferent—now as then it's only possible
to touch lightly and never both at once.
                                        Intolerance
follows. A better lover. You draw into your husk
and find a snake-eyed face smiling from the water.
It wears a hood of green fir. If only those lips,
you begin to say, would part in something other than mockery.
You throw water over your left shoulder—find you are
no longer Narcissus but a tree frog. Orange rosettes checker
your right side, while the left is flawed
by tattoos.
               The USDA mark will wear off
but also the skin. You are corn again,
as you have feared, apprehension weaves, but you look
in front of you—a gigantic blue windmill-like crane
carries buckets of men through an oculus in the clouds,
only to dump them at its peak. Not everyone falls,
a few fly, a few cling to the bucket for a free ride down.
But most tumble like cherry blossoms in a high wind.
They are exceedingly small, dressed in business suits
which flutter in marvellous disarray as the occupants
squawk and fall.

On the ground some are thrown apart
like quail caught in mowing blades. Others,
more comfortable, are equipped with travel guides.
From a conveyer belt apartment buildings are lifted
and stacked like egg cartons. What is going on,
you mutter, but everyone is doing what he can.
The machine does not seem to have a driver
and the maplike blueprints piled all over the place
impede progress at every turn. The intricate metallic
fingers that pluck materials for the baskets
break down in fields unfolded like giant comic strips.
Whoever is not
stripping trees, or foraging moleward beneath grassy quilts,
seems to be standing around as you are—in awe
and cheering for a phalanx sent out to reset traffic lights.
These have at the corners baskets of hornets
that fly in teletype formations and molest
everyone. The stock market is on the way out,
in fact it levitates. Bingo, someone calls
—hazards and lizards, glowworms and wrong turns
explode in a rainbow of fertilizer. Cleopatra
is carried in rolled up in a 12 foot tortilla.
The lattice work builds,
humming. You notice
iridescent nets cast everywhere—you are in tears
but cannot say why—the nests are woven, in the park
and in the parking lot. You go to a gazebo
for a glass of port. Yet something
hangs in the air—like negative mistletoe, or
foggy fireworks, it hangs there—then disappears.

Music

of blood stone garnet
worn at the throat,
melody shaped in
rays of pointed light
—your hand shielded,
made cups of rhyme—
cones on a poplar branch
that flowered before
all who were open to
its radiant measure.
Each phrase wove
layers of imagined contour
—or stunned unfolded,
as if a voice unaccustomed
to give anything but pleasure
had been injured. To become
free again it spun
a song richer than all others
—shoots of melody anchored
a lattice work of sight;
from it green trails
of harmony gathered
around you like a charm.

after rehearing a tape
of Robin Blaser reading

Love's Haze

Light touched foliage of
caress—turning our lives
so we do not or may not

unturn them. Going to meet you
—there are spots of unclear density,
I am not sure whether I go headlong

or am kept back. Knots of stranded
feeling unfold pools, I have feared
quicksand, continuing to love

is travel in a pleasant boat
over other waters of whose depth
and bottom I am not sure

—whether guided or propelled,
it does not matter, we move parallel
together—at times a watery

voluptuousness reaches to pull me
away, or take you. I sweat—
hooked out of sleep beyond knowing

it's not failure, but how far
—vertigo. To a cool suddenness
your touch is a warm wind, sunny

to my grumbling, I have no sunglasses,
I've lost the map, you are a pleasure
that makes me furious—all stops there

and I am postmarked to myself,
as if I had only begun to breathe
or know a delightful care

in getting along with someone lovely
—knowing you well enough to share
love, not throw it away, build

from remorse the negative equal to
hours spent hectic or dreaming
—let them go, come back, I look

for you to return—
you're ahead of me, not waiting
—our movement continues,

soft luminous spots unfeather,
their subtlety in arrangement
matched by difficulty in following

or surety in finding again
those patches of brilliant fever,
I often wander in, lost on

a light giddy trail—I don't
bother where. Yet it warms. Worn
as something mine and familiar

I am startled to find no restraint,
I want to travel on the mysterious lake
—or firmly tread toward that face

of mine which would destroy love. It is
almost gone, loving has so often said
'you're empty' and been right.

Through an elliptical door
we move to unshielded rhythms.
We are sitting on a terrace where the wind

fools at the hem of your coat.
You have some weird flowers in hand
—we're laughing as we begin to walk, you swirl

gold and violet of desire's cloak,
folds of mistaken and right-taken starts,
threads from love's fine loom.

2 September 1970

The Camera

I've taken down my figure of the moon
—there is too much loneliness in poetry.

As if the waterlilies in the aquarium
bloomed upside down—visible through glass walls

the roots like small hydroelectric plants
foraged the air. Are they signaling?

You come back from putting money in the jukebox,
but of the seven songs you played four turn out

the same. A few people dance. You get another coin
—but *Der Rosenkavalier* wasn't there in the first place.

You end up tearful over an illegible postcard.
Good-bye to the whale. You are at your prayers again

—revising them. The electric puttering carried up
a funnel of light. But was the camera loaded?

The facts unscrew, turn open like fans. Light leaks
out of them enough to let you see those people

you run to greet have begun to run toward you.
You're out of focus when you meet, not sure

what to say. Everyone is formal, then embracing
around an outdoor urn of forget-me-nots. Words stain,

they sail above us like kites with wet satin tails,
oval saucers in a clear sky. Then snow, parting,

as it gets closer, into shapes of fruit, to grow
in sacred trees. One hangs there and will not fade out.